"If money can't buy you love,
then maybe bitcoin can."

Anonymous - 2021

CONTENTS

About the author

James has been a pioneer of digital technology the internet since its early days. Currently Media Strategy director for WPP. In his earlier career, he founded three highly successful digital agencies and has also held the roles of Chief Digital, Data, and Strategy Officer for several large companies.

When not indulging in all things crypto-related, he is also a skilled practitioner in the ancient arts of Origami and Kung Fu (in which he holds a black belt.)

So, let's begin with a joke.

A joke called DOGECOIN, to be precise.

Back in 2013, which represents a lifetime in crypto years, two former video game software engineers at IBM, Billy Markus, and Jackson Palmer decided to launch their own cryptocurrency, which they called Dogecoin, named after the virtual currency, used in the Nintendo game Animal Crossing.

Their original intention was to create what they described as the cryptocurrency for sillies, or in other words, a joke, intended to poke fun at Bitcoin, and I am assuming bitcoin given the distinct lack of different cryptocurrencies in existence at the time.

Fast forward to 2015 and faced with being out of work and a growing annoyance that no one seemed to get the joke, Billy sold all his Dogecoin to buy himself a car, an excellent second-hand Honda civic.

So, what, you ask is wrong with that?

Well, when you consider that as of mid-December 2021, the market value or capitalization of Dogecoin sits at around $28.2Billion and recently has been as high as $85billion, then you start to realize that in the history of bad decisions, Billy's decision making is right up there amongst the best, or perhaps the worst.

And perhaps even more ironically, on December 14, 2021, Elon Musk, CEO of what is now the world's most automotive company Tesla, stated that they would now be accepting Dogecoin as a means of payment.

And Dogecoin is not alone, it seems.

SHIBA INU, a digital token or currency, initially started in 2020 with the sole intention of being the anti-Dogecoin, is itself now worth $29Billion based on its current market capitalization.

And it gets even crazier still, with 2021 having seen a flood of new Shib in tribute tokens emerge, SHIBZILLA, FLOKI INU, and SHIBORG INU being some of note, while not to be outdone, Dogecoin has also sparked its own, tribute tokens such as BABYDOGE and DOGELON MARS amongst them.

While this might all seem like madness, and in some regards it is, it also begs the obvious question: What the hell is going on?

How can something that started as a joke now be worth the same as major corporations that have been in existence for many, many years?

Welcome to the crazy world of cryptocurrency!

While this world may seem not just crazy but almost unfathomable on first observation, it is really very straightforward to understand.

And that is because, at its heart, cryptocurrency is nothing more than a currently unfolding story composed of three simple and very human chapters, those being GOLD, GREED, and GOOD.

However, before we dive into the story starting with the story of gold, it is worth spending a little time arming you with some of the critical language and terms used in the cryptocurrency world, as like many things born from technology, the jargon surrounding it can be somewhat confusing if not explained in advance.

Now, of course, if you are already well versed in the language and culture of cryptocurrency, and know your blockchain from your VeChain, then do head straight on to chapter one - GOLD.

But if not, then before we begin the story, let us take a quick tour of some essential language and phrases that will help you both make sense of crypto and sound like a deep expert at dinner parties too!

When it comes to the world of cryptocurrency and its current set of language and terminology, it is very much a case of 'qeylIS.'

If you are a star trek fan or Trekkie to use the correct terminology, you will recognize that qeylIS is Klingon for cryptocurrency.

However, if you are not like me, it makes little sense without the explanation just offered.

And the same is true of the cryptocurrency space, and it possesses a language set more befitting of another galaxy or planet than the one we currently reside upon.

So, let's address this by starting with the actual words of CRYPTO and CRYPTOCURRENCY themselves.

CRYPTOCURRENCY refers to a distinct digital currency or store of value, or in even more straightforward language, a form of digital money.

CRYPTO, on the other hand, while in some applications, is used as a shortening of CRYPTOCURRENCY, is also increasingly used as a more expansive phrase for the wider digital universe and ecosystem developing around cryptocurrencies, including areas such as the currently in vogue' metaverse.' A little confusing, I grant you.

Turning our attention back to specific cryptocurrencies for a moment, within these, we find two distinct types, COINS and TOKENS.

COINS are digital currencies that exist on their own data infrastructure or blockchains (don't worry, I will cover that in a moment), while TOKENS will use an already existing infrastructure or blockchains and, as a result, are easier to establish and increasingly more prevalent.

Bitcoin is an example of a COIN, hence the name, while SHIB INU, mentioned earlier in this book, is a TOKEN that utilizes the already existing ETHEREUM blockchain.

You will also increasingly hear the word ALT-COIN used, meaning nothing more than an alternative to BITCOIN (the original and current benchmark digital currency). However, perhaps somewhat annoyingly, the term ALT-COIN is often used to describe coins and tokens alike in the present landscape.

The BLOCKCHAIN mentioned above, and a word you will often hear in the world of crypto, is simply a decentralized database where transactions for a cryptocurrency are stored and validated.

The critical word here is decentralized, meaning that no one single user or computer can validate alone; instead, it uses multiple unconnected users or validation points to store and validate, which in theory means it cannot be interfered with or altered.

Sometimes, you will also hear the phrases' decentralized ledger' and the '51% rule.

A DENCETRALISED LEDGER is just another way of saying a decentralized database.

The 51% RULE refers to the simple fact that no one person or institution can control 51% or more of a digital currency if the decentralized principle maintains its integrity.

Next, we will cover a term that has had more than its fair share of use and media coverage in recent weeks - the NFT.

The term NFT stands for NON-FUNGIBLE TOKEN.

While that might sound super complex, it is just another way of describing something as unique or one of a kind.

Cryptocurrencies, be them coins are tokens, are considered fungible, and one can easily be replicated with another identical item.

For example, a BITCOIN is fungible as each bitcoin is not unique and can be replaced by another identical one.

Non-fungible items, such as a digital picture of a crypto punk or a similar digital artwork, are defined as fungible or unique and cannot be replicated or replaced with another identical copy.

However, in terms of recording and validating their uniqueness, they utilize a blockchain in the same way as cryptocurrency tokens, with many currently using the Ethereum blockchain platform.

Okay, so now let's look at buying and selling crypto currencies with more essential terms and elements of knowledge.

An EXCHANGE is a place where you can buy and sell crypto-currencies and swap them for others.

There are two types of exchanges currently in operation.

Firstly, you have the more mainstream scaled exchanges: Coinbase, Crypto.com Robinhood, and Binance are examples of these.

These platforms allow you to buy cryptocurrencies with mainstream legal tender (often called FIAT) via existing bank accounts or credit cards and transfer money out into traditional bank accounts as FIAT currencies.

As cryptocurrencies start to become more mainstream and these platforms increasingly find themselves the subject of more regulation and scrutiny, they are increasingly just able to offer the more mainstream, less volatile COINS and TOKENS to be bought and sold.

They also tend to be owned and controlled as single entitles, much like mainstream financial organizations and banks in the traditional financial world.

The second type of exchange is a DECENTRALISED EXCHANGE, also sometimes called DeFi Exchanges in deference to being a decentralized form of financial platform.

As the name suggests, these tend to be decentralized in ownership and development, operating as a collective of often unconnected individuals, much like how Linux works in the software world.

Most of these decentralized exchanges allow you to swap one crypto for another instead of FIAT-based money and are built on either the Binance blockchain (known as BSC20) or the Ethereum blockchain (known as ERC20).

This distinction is crucial because you cannot currently send ERC blockchain tokens to a BSC blockchain and vice versa - so depending on the platform, you need to own or already have Binance coin (BNB) or Etheruem (ETH) available to use them.

Current examples of DeFi exchanges are Pancake swap which uses the Binance blockchain, and Uniswap, which uses Ethereum.

As you have probably worked out, these exchanges are far less regulated than the mainstream ones and are where you can trade in the new emerging cryptocurrencies.

However, it should also be noted that these types of exchanges present a much riskier environment, best avoided until you have cut your teeth on the more mainstream platforms and exchanges, well, at least in my opinion.

Once you have purchased your cryptocurrency, you will need somewhere secure to store it, as even though it is now digital money, it is still representative of your hard-earned cash.

The first option is to store your cryptocurrency on the exchange you bought it from.

(This option only exists with the mainstream platforms and not on the DeFi ones, where you will need an existing wallet to use them but more of that in a moment.)

While it might seem like a sensible approach to store your newly acquired cryptocurrency in the place you purchased it doing so is not a particularly good idea.

There are two reasons why this is the case.

Firstly, despite the best efforts of the exchange platforms, including offering security features such as two-factor authentication, the reality is that the exchanges are still open to hacking. And sadly, as the crypto market has exploded, so too has the frequency of such attacks.

And the second reason you should never keep any purchased cryptocurrency on exchanges is also the most important.

Even though you have paid for your cryptocurrency with your money, you have purchased it using the keys or IDs owned by the exchange in the first instance.

Therefore, until you actively change this by moving your cryptocurrency off the exchange and assigning it to a key you own, it remains owned by the exchange platform you have used.

Now anyone looking for a cautionary tale to back up my assertion needs to look no further than the curious case of Quadriga CX.

Now the subject of a rather excellent documentary film made by the discovery channel, Quadriga CX was a Canadian bitcoin exchange platform whose founder seemingly died in mysterious circumstances.

Following his death, it then emerged that he had all the keys to around $250million worth of Bitcoin stored on the exchange had also vanished, meaning that none of it could be accessed or retrieved by its rightful owners.

As a result of such stories and the obvious security risk, most cryptocurrency purchasers move their COINS or TOKENS to what is known as a crypto wallet.

A cryptocurrency WALLET is, as it sounds, a digital wallet in which to store your money, much in the same way you would keep analog cash in a physical wallet or purse.

Also, any wallet you choose should be **NON-CUSTODIAL** - i.e., the wallet does not own your crypto keys, and if not, that should act as a big red flag, and as to why? See the Quadriga CX case above.

You can use two types of wallets: a SOFTWARE WALLET and what is known as a HARDWARE or COLD WALLET.

Regardless of type, all wallets are secured with something called a SEED PHRASE, a random 12 or 24-word combination that is needed to access or recover your wallet and digital currency IDs, which it contains.

A software wallet is, as it sounds, a wallet that exists entirely on your PC: Mac or mobile device.

Examples of popular software wallets would be Trust wallet or Metamask.

However, while generally secure, the software-only approach means that the currency keys or ID remain on the device, meaning they are still open to hacking attacks and can never be considered 100% secure.

As a result, many people choose to store their cryptocurrency on what is known as a HARDWARE WALLET.

Again, as the name implies, this is an actual hardware device, USB-like in appearance, that you interact with to use your currency keys and interact with your cryptocurrency.

The device never goes online or connects to the internet; hence, it is sometimes also referred to as a COLD WALLET.

It offers by far the most secure way to store cryptocurrency and, for anyone with serious investments, an essential item to have.

Examples of popular hardware wallets would be the Ledger Nano wallets or Trezor devices.

HARDWARE WALLETS are by far the most secure way to store and transact cryptocurrency and anyone serious about investing, especially for the long term, in my opinion, needs to utilize one, if only for peace of mind.

Given that you're probably wondering what has happened to the promised story of gold greed and good, we will conclude this short education piece with two final but critical terms: PROOF OF WORK and PROOF OF STAKE.

These terms relate to how transactions are validated and processed on the blockchain and have important implications for the future of cryptocurrency.

Proof of work" and "proof of stake" are the two primary consensus mechanisms cryptocurrencies use to verify new transactions, add them to the blockchain, and create new tokens.

PROOF OF WORK, first pioneered by Bitcoin, uses mining to achieve those goals, while PROOF OF STAKE is employed by the latest Cryptocurrencies such as Cardano XLM and XRP, which use staking to accomplish the same thing.

But if that still sounds a little confusing, then let's explain a little further.

Decentralized cryptocurrency networks need to ensure that nobody spends the same money twice without a central authority like Visa or PayPal in the middle.

To do this, networks use a "consensus mechanism," which allows all the computers in a crypto network to agree about which transactions are legitimate.

Proof of work is the original crypto consensus mechanism, first used by Bitcoin, and often you will also hear it referred to as CRYPTO MINING.

The reason it's called "proof of work" is because Proof-of-work blockchains are secured and verified by virtual miners worldwide racing to be the first to solve a math puzzle.

The winner updates the blockchain with the latest verified transactions and is rewarded by the network with a predetermined amount of crypto.

While proof of work or mining is a proven, robust way of maintaining a secure decentralized blockchain, it is also a very energy-intensive process that can have trouble scaling to accommodate the vast number of transactions blockchains can generate.

To address this, newer second-generation blockchains have developed an alternative model - the PROOF OF STAKE approach.

In a proof of stake system, staking serves a similar function to proof of work as the process by which a network participant gets selected to add the latest batch of transactions to the blockchain and earn some crypto in exchange.

However, proof of stake blockchains, instead of allowing miners to compete to validate transactions, employs a network of "validators" who contribute — or "stake" — their crypto in exchange for a chance to validate new transactions, update updates the blockchain, and earn rewards.

The crucial differences between the two are that proof-of-stake blockchains don't require miners to spend electricity on duplicative processes (competing to solve the same puzzle). Hence, proof of stake can operate with substantially lower resource consumption and more speed and efficiency.

Okay, so that is now hopefully enough language and insights for now.

If nothing else, you can now sound like a true expert at dinner parties if someone, God forbid, starts a discussion around the benefits of proof of stake versus proof of work!

So, without further ado, let's get back to our story and start with chapter one - GOLD.

CHAPTER ONE

GOLD

So, chapter one, GOLD is, in essence, the story of Bitcoin - the original and still (at least in 2021) dominant cryptocurrency.

On January 3, 2009, Bitcoin came into being when a gentleman called Satoshi Nakamoto mined the genesis block of bitcoin (block number 0), earning 50 bitcoins.

It may or may not surprise you that bitcoin was not the first attempt at digital cash or currency, nor was it unique in design or origin.

The idea of what we would now call the blockchain' originated in 1992 when the idea that solutions to computational puzzles could have some value was first proposed by cryptographers Cynthia Dwork and Adam Back then picked up the idea in 1997, who used it to develop HASHCASH as a proof of work scheme for spam control.

This subsequently evolved into more specific attempts at digital currency by Wei Dai and Nick Szabo, who created b-money and bit-gold using hashcash as the proof of work algorithm.

However, perhaps because the world was not ready, and indeed that was true of the internet, it wasn't until the arrival of bitcoin that the idea began to catch on.

However, while we now know what inspired bitcoins creator Satoshi Nakamoto and what he based his work on, we know little else about him, and since its inception, there has been much mystery surrounding who he is.

And the mystery deepened when On April 28, 2011, the bitcoin creator disappeared after stepping down from his role as project lead, which has since led to April 28 being designated Satoshi Disappear Day in the cryptocurrency world.

Since then, efforts have continued to try and identify him, with the following candidates being of note.

First up, we have Hal Finney, a pre-bitcoin cryptographic pioneer.

Interestingly, he was the first person (besides Nakamoto himself) to use the software and lived a few blocks from a man named 'Dorian Satoshi Nakamoto.

However, after much investigation, Forbes journalist Andy Greenberg stated that Finney's denials of being Satoshi were, in his opinion, trustworthy.

Similarly, a high-profile March 6, 2014, article in Newsweek by journalist Leah Goodman identified Dorian Prentice Satoshi Nakamoto, a Japanese American man living in California as the bitcoin founder.

However, following a subsequent media frenzy, including reporters camping out near his house and chasing him by car, Dorian Nakamoto denied all connection to bitcoin, although still to this day, when you search for Satoshi, it is Dorian's picture that appears.

And the theories continue to emerge, ranging from the idea that Satoshi is maybe a foreign government or revolutionary group looking to destabilize the United States government, through to the notion that bitcoin was gifted to us by aliens, which as well as being the most dramatic is my favorite one too.

And while a more credible claim made recently by the world's second-richest man and Tesla CEO, Elon Musk, that hyper-secretive cryptocurrency expert Nick Szabo could be the original Satoshi Nakamoto, as to the truth or reality of who or what Satoshi Nakamoto is, we may never know.

But what we do know for sure is that the first-ever consumer transaction using bitcoin occurred on May 22, 2010, in Florida.

This occurred when Florida-based Laszlo Hanyecz decided that he was hungry and traded 10,000 Bitcoins to get two pizzas from his local Pap John's local pizza store.

Now obviously, back in 2010, no one, especially not your local pizza store, was accepting cryptocurrency as payment.

Therefore, as you do in such situations, Laszlo turned to the internet and found someone willing to order and pay for his Pizza, sending them 10,000 bitcoins in return.

Now alongside the previously mentioned decision of Billy Markus to trade his Dogecoin for a Honda civic, this sits right up there in the top two terrible cryptocurrency decisions, for the simple fact that at today's valuation (2021), those two Pizza's costs him $287million.

So legendary has this become that crypto fans have named and celebrated May 22 as Bitcoin Pizza Day ever since!

Now bitcoin has come a long way since then, and indeed, you can now easily buy fast food with it (more of that later).

And today, bitcoin sits atop a rapidly growing cryptocurrency market, which at the end of 2021 was nudging $3trillion in value.

And in that rapidly evolving world, bitcoin is increasingly being seen as both a form of digital money or currency and a store of value or, to put it another way, a form of digital gold, hence the title of this chapter.

And the gold analogy, I believe, is an excellent one for two key reasons.

Firstly, bitcoin is increasingly being used as a store of value, especially in uncertain economic times resulting from the global COVID-19 pandemic in 2020 & 2021.

And even when compared to gold, whose benefits for storing value and wealth over time, its current performance has been significantly better in recent years.

Across 2021, $1 invested in gold in January would at the start of December be worth $0.96, while $1 invested in bitcoin, even with a significant market drop occurring in November, would be worth $2.58

And while I would consider it an unfair comparison, if you extend that date range back to October 2009 when bitcoin first arrived, your $1 of gold would be worth $1.56, while your bitcoin would be now worth $68,417,028!

So clearly, it is not hard to understand why people increasingly see Bitcoin as a form of digital gold based on its economics. Still, the second reason that gold is a great analogy is that, like good old-fashioned gold, you can mine for bitcoin too.

Earlier in this book, I covered the proof of work concept around which bitcoin operates in more detail, but I didn't allude to the romantic element this idea brings.

Just as in the days of old with the gold rush, the opportunity to mine this digital gold is seemingly open to all, old or young, and with it comes the romantic notion of wealth and reward.

However, at least today, the reality is that you are extremely unlikely to get rich doing so, much like actual gold mining.

To even stand a chance of making a sustainable living from bitcoin or cryptocurrency mining, you need access to ever-increasing (and hence expensive) computational power.

Now at the risk of steeping a little too far into the technological complexity of crypto mining, it is helpful to understand how this works.

Transactions are added to the blockchain or decentralized database of transactions in groups or blocks.

These blocks are added to the blockchain by whichever computer in the network can first find a unique key – the answer to a mathematical problem first.

The first computer to verify the transaction and find the key is rewarded with a certain amount of Bitcoin (for example, the reward was 6.25 BTC in 2020).

This key is an algorithm-generated, 64-digit hexadecimal number (or "hash") that is less than or equal to the target hash, upon which is built the most recent block added to the blockchain.

In this way, every new block validates every subsequent block, creating the blockchain and thus the name blockchain.

Because this mining is done using powerful computers capable of generating thousands, millions, and even billions of hashes per second, it requires large amounts of electricity.

As the value of Bitcoin rises and the blockchain network grows, the difficulty of solving each cryptographic problem grows, and alongside this, more people are incentivized to become miners.

And with this comes the need for more and more computing power, machines capable of generating thousands, millions, and even billions of hashes per second.

And all this ultimately, yes, you guessed it, requires large amounts of electricity.

And the output of this is a dual impact.

Firstly, it increasingly excludes everyday users, eroding the decentralized basis of the blockchain (remember the 50%), returning more control to larger wealthy organizations and even governments, yes including China.

And seconding it represents an increasingly significant Achilles' heel for bitcoin, its environmental impact as more and more energy is used.

And this impact is significant.

At the end of 2021, it is estimated the Bitcoin network consumes about 116 terawatts per hour or 116 trillion watts per year.

To put that in context, that's about 0.5% of the total electricity in the world—more electricity consumption than in many countries!

And while many bitcoin advocates will argue that mining's electricity consumption isn't that bad compared to the environmental toll of global data centers and digital banking at 0.8% and that, more importantly, much of the energy used is renewable, according to the Cambridge Center for Alternative Finance, only about 39% of bitcoin mining is today powered by actual renewable energy sources.

And finally, add into this the fact that on December 12, 2021, bitcoin block #714,032 was mined at 23:26 UTC, rewarded its miner with 6.25 BTC, indicating that 90% of all bitcoins have now been excavated, and scarcity becomes not just a blessing, but also a potential curse too.

And if these issues themselves were not enough, bitcoin is also increasingly suffering from the fact that it is increasingly old technology in cryptocurrency years.

To give that some context, bitcoin can handle seven transactions per second, while a next generation blockchain platform using proof of stake, for example, stellar lumens (XLM), can deliver one thousand.

Even more significantly, while bitcoin takes around ten minutes to create a new block, XLM can achieve this task in a mere five seconds.

Given this, it is then unsurprising that when one of Ukraine's oldest commercial banks, Tascombank, announced plans to test a digital version of their sovereign currency, the Hryvnia, they announced that it will be built and tested on the Stellar network.

Now, of course, many crypto experts will immediately point to Bitcoin's Lightning Network as the answer to this.

As a quick overview, the lightning network is a second layer technology applied to bitcoin that uses micropayment channels to scale its blockchain's capability to conduct transactions more efficiently.

Indeed, as we end 2021, there are a record number of global computers (roughly 18,000 "nodes") operating this Lightning Network.

However, despite this apparent upgrade, several fundamental challenges with scaling bitcoin this way remain.

If one was being rude, one could liken it to putting lipstick on a pig, granted a precious pig.

So, for me, this allied to the problems with proof of work or mining as its model, along with the fact that supply is finite at just 21 million, means that as a functional cryptocurrency for everyone, bitcoin may have a limited future.

And so, while it may be considered a controversial viewpoint, for me, its future role will be much more as a store of wealth or benchmark of value in the same what that gold operates.

And potentially, it could even overtake gold in this regard with a panel of 50 top cryptocurrency experts, brought together by Forbes magazine in mid-2021, even predicting that it could reach £5million per bitcoin by 2030.

And as the specter of growing inflation looms in a post covid world, more and more people are turning to bitcoin instead of gold.

Interestingly, this includes several countries, which I will go into later when considering the story's GOOD portion.

But bitcoin also performs another even more important role for my money, or maybe that should be crypto.

And that is as a proof of concept, the trailblazer that has more than proved that decentralized cryptocurrencies can and do work and acting as the industry poster child.

Without bitcoin performing this role, likely, I would not be writing this book, nor would you have any interest in reading it, as cryptocurrency would most likely not be what it is today.

However, what I don't think bitcoin alone can explain, is the current frenzy and explosion in other altcoins, which now stand at well over a thousand and are growing daily.

Instead, to explain that we need to look to a different further dynamic or driver alongside the emergence of bitcoin.

And that dynamic is GREED, the subject of my next chapter.

For me, one of the critical drivers I believe for the reason explosion digital money or cryptocurrency, is something very non-digital and analog, good old fashioned human greed.

In 1987, Gordon Gecko, a composite character in the 1987 film Wall Street, based on the real-life Wall Street trader Ivan Boesky declared that "Greed is good."

And while many would argue that ever since the world has frowned upon such advice and declarations, it now seems that greed is making a comeback with the emergence of cryptocurrencies and is indeed good once again.

You only must speed a few minutes browsing social media platforms, especially TikTok, to see multiple posts declaring 'These cryptocurrencies will make you a millionaire' and showing images of luxury, Lamborghinis, and lifestyles of the rich and famous.

Yes, you too can be a millionaire or even a billionaire. All you must do is invest in cryptocurrencies, and technically, these posts are factually correct.

And that is simply because, for just a few pounds or dollars, you can purchase millions or billions of exotic sound cryptocurrencies.

What about some SPACE GRIME?

For just $5, you can own 402billion tokens!

Not really into space?

Then what about some BABYDOGE or SHIBZILLA? For currently just $5, you can be a billionaire in both.

Don't like dogs or space, then what about some CATGIRL tokens?

Yet again, for a mere $10, you can be a CATGIRL billionaire, and yes, I already am, thanks!

Still not for you?

Then maybe the cryptocurrency for you is MONGOOSE COIN.

This token emerged overnight on December 9, 2021, in response to a comment by Brad Sherman, a Democratic Congressman from California, who joked, "What could Mongoose Coin do to CryptoCoin?" explaining how he just made it up. Mongoose coin, that is.

And made it up he had because, by December 9, MONGOOSE COIN had become real, with over $2.8million of transactions already recorded!

But assuming the desire to be a millionaire is currently restricted to that being measured in traditional FIAT currencies. It is more the promise or allure that such posts and cryptocurrencies offer that is significant here.

And beyond the realms of social media, we also see more mainstream media covering stories of people who have found life-changing wealth by investing in cryptocurrency.

For example, consider the case of Rob, a 35-year-old, now former supermarket warehouse manager from the North of England, a story covered by many highly regarded publications, including Forbes magazine.

Rob began researching cryptocurrencies in northern England in late 2020 and early 2021.

He aimed to modestly grow the tens of thousands of dollars in savings he had built with his partner to create a better future for their young son.

While researching, Rob came across the previously mentioned SHIB INU token, a cryptocurrency "meme" token built on the Ethereum blockchain launched in August 2020 by someone who calls themself Ryoshi.

After reading Ryoshi's 'woofpaper,' a play on the term white paper, which explained the Shiba Inu philosophy, Rob decided to invest $8000 of his yearly $6800 earnings into the token.

Fast forward to mid-2021, and his $8000 has turned into several million, allowing him to retire into the lap of luxury.

And why not consider the case of Davinci Jeremie.

Famous for making and posting a YouTube video in 2013, urging everyone to invest at least $1 in bitcoin at that time.

And it is safe to assume he took his advice and invested more than $1, as his social media feed now shows him constantly surrounded by helicopters and private jets or onboard yachts in the ocean.

Incidentally, Davinci now seems to advocate taking a similar action regarding XRP. You heard it here first!

Yes, as I said, good old-fashioned greed and material wealth seem to have returned with the advent of cryptocurrency, and where dreams of wealth are supplemented by fear of missing out (FOMO) to create a solid and powerful driver for growth.

The reality is that many of the currently available cryptocurrencies possess no intrinsic value or worth.

These are known in crypto circles as MEME or SHITCOINS; tokens launched with no real utility or defined purpose.

Some of these currencies have unsurprisingly turned out to be elaborate Ponzi schemes, or HONEY TRAPS, to use the correct crypto terminology.

.

These are cryptocurrencies that use smart contracts designed to allow you to invest money but from which you then cannot withdraw.

And then, when enough value or liquidity is built up, those behind the scheme extract this in one fell swoop, known as a RUG PULL in crypto terminology.

An example of this was SQUID, a digital token seemingly inspired and linked to the popular South Korean Netflix series Squid Games.

Squid, which marketed itself as a "play-to-earn cryptocurrency," saw its price soar by thousands of percent to hit $2,856 per token at one point.

However, SQUID came with an even higher price, which was the inability of those investing to extract their money.

And once the currency hit around $1.9Billion, those behind the scam pulled the token's liquidity and sent the value crashing by 99.99% in seconds.

In other words, it was a classic rug pull and one that saw those behind it make millions as a result but blinded by social media hype and the perceived association to the hit Netflix series, seemingly blinded from the truth.

Similarly, another scam token MANDO, named after the hit Disney show Mandalorian, emerged earlier in 2021.

So convincing was this scheme, it was even able to dupe a famous TikTok influencer, Matt Lorion, known for his content about trading, finance, and cryptocurrency.

Indeed, Mr. Lorion, who personally invested $10,000 into the scam token, was so beside himself for promoting it to his TikTok audience, that on March 13, 2021, he publicly apologized for the scam in a posted TikTok video to the same followers to whom he had promoted the potential of Mando just one week previously.

And these are just two prime examples of these pump-and-dump schemes, where once the honey pot is filled to the brim before the rug is well and truly pulled.

In fact, according to estimates by Ciphertrace Cryptocurrency Intelligence, between January and July 2021 alone, investors were duped out of some $113million by way of such rug pull schemes.

There are, of course, ways and means to identify the legitimacy of such schemes, or the rather the lack, including the rather excellent POOCOIN.APP, a site where you can check a token's various dynamics, including the incoming and critically outgoing trades, and which offers a fighting chance of avoiding such crypto Ponzi schemes, if not a cast-iron guarantee.

But it would be unfair to label all these cryptocurrencies Ponzi schemes because, in reality, most of them are more akin to good old-fashioned snake oil, be it digital snake oil for the crypto age.

Despite the evident lack of obvious utility or application for many of these meme coins, the momentum and interest around them continue to escalate and grow at pace, as does the collective financial value.

And whether the news behind them is fake or not, and a lot of it is sadly fake, or at least fanciful, people seem not to care.

Any concerns or doubts are quickly extinguished with a few images of Lamborghinis and the odd yacht, and all expertly curated by the crypto snake oil salesmen.

And some of these snake oil salesmen are, in fact, very famous and entirely credible.

Mention Dogecoin, and Elon Musk, the entrepreneur behind Tesla and SpaceX, tends to emerge.

A single one-word tweet from Elon has been proven to alter the price of Dogecoin, and that also holds for non-meme coins like Bitcoin.

As a case in point, on April 27, 2021, Elon tweeted "one word - DOGE" and sent the price of Dogecoin soaring by 20%, while more recently, on December 14, after tweeting 'Tesla will make some merch buyable with Doge & see how it goes,' the price of DOGE again shot up by 30% or so.

And talking of premium snake oil sales, welcome to the even crazier world of NFT's or non-fungible tokens to use the full name, which has taken the current greed dynamics around cryptocurrencies to a whole new level.

From rocks to bored apes, crypto kitties, and on to cyberpunks, the world of cryptocurrency and beyond has seemingly gone NFT mad in the last few months, again supercharged by social media and the wider media in general.

And it is not just the crazy crypto kids or startups getting involved in this either, far from it.

At the end of August 2021, the payments processor VISA confirmed it had bought a "CryptoPunk," NFT for nearly $150,000 in Ethereum, something which turned out to be a wise move given that by the end of September 2021, similar NFT's were selling for up to $11 million each!

And even the most unlikely of brands are getting involved too.

Charmain, the purveyor of toilet paper, recently released its collection of toilet paper themed NFTs, cleverly branded as non-fungible toilet paper.

At the same time, Taco Bell, the famous American fast-food chain, pre-ceded them by removing its limited-edition range of TACO GIF's all of which sold out in 25 minutes.

(And yes, it has crossed my mind, as I am sure it just did yours, that perhaps the two could somehow be related.)

And not to be left out in the cold, as with the emergence of bitcoin years earlier, that other stalwart of fast-food Pizza has also been getting in on the act.

Most notably, Pizza Hut Canada created a pixelated NFT pizza, putting it on sale for just 0.0001 ETH ($0.18) to make it affordable (like a bite of Pizza), only to see it rapidly; rise to $9000!

And even the humble potato chip (or crisp if you are from the UK) has gotten in on the NFT act, too, with Pringles releasing their CryptoCrisp in 2021, a collection of 50 NFT's created by artist Vasya Kolotusha.

Now while it might be effortless to dismiss all of this as madness, or at the very least as just a craze, while using the word bandwagon, what we are witnessing is disruption and democratization to an area, ART which hasn't seen the like since Andy Warhol decided to paint his lunch.

And it would be fair to say that in a few short months, the application of cryptocurrency to the artwork through NFT's has already turned the world of art on its head, where anyone armed with ideas and an iPhone can be the next DaVinci.

And that even includes my wonderful daughter Hollie, currently aged thirteen and a bit.

When faced with a recent art project, instead of turning to the traditional route of sticky-backed plastic glitter and glue, we instead turned to the world of NFT's for inspiration, resulting in the Crypto Bond collection on opensea.io

(If you are interested, you can see the collection here - https://tinyurl.com/cryptobond007)

But it is not just the art world being turned on its head by cryptocurrency and the NFT revolution.

The gaming world is also being disrupted and fundamentally reinvented at an ever-increasing velocity.

In recent years, the gaming industry (along with music and film) has already undergone significant disruption and transformation with the arrival of online gaming and digital downloads and formats.

In addition, the emergence of new subscription models through titles such as horizon zero dawn was further disrupting the commercial model away from buying titles upfront before commencing play.

Now added to this existing disruption, the impact of NFT's and crypto, I believe, is significant on two levels.

Firstly, NFT's are increasingly becoming the content or elements within a game. Whether this is your character or simply clothing that it wears, these are now becoming the domain of the NFT.

And for sure, that would certainly help explain why Nike recently purchased NFT fashion and collectibles startup RTFKT.

But it doesn't stop there. Almost every element of a game can lend itself to becoming an NFT.

From land through to houses, cars, and even furniture in games or virtual worlds, the NFT now becomes the content.

And in this brave new world of gaming, what is a game?

It can be anything and everything in the world of NFT's and the metaverse.

Consider, if you will, the curious example of the CRYPTO HOTEL.

Perhaps not a game in the old sense of the word, with a beginning and end, The Crypto Hotel is a unique virtual hotel with 100 rooms, all of which enjoy a great view over the open sea, the beach, the pool area, and the Crypto golf course.

And yes, you have guessed it pretty much everything in the hotel, from the guests through to the mini-bar shacks (and we assume over-priced as always), are NFT's available for purchase.

But why pay to play only?

One of the bit components in evidence around a lot of the new NFT gaming platforms and environments is a reversal of the pay-to-play model to one of play to earn, which is very much as it sounds.

While many people currently earn a living by playing games, such as professional e-sports participants, the arrival of NFT's into gaming brings with it a promise that playing the games they love can be a suitable career path for anyone.

Historically even as gaming has grown to become the world's largest media category, all game-based economic activity has mainly remained centralized, giving developers and publishers the rights to everything going on within their games.

That means that most players themselves have few ways to share in the value generated by this industry.

However, with the arrival of NFT's and the push to decentralization, these so-called 'play-to-earn' games allow players to earn and own digital assets that they can then sell outside of the game at their discretion.

The true innovation here lies in the decentralized integrity and security of these digital items, which—for the first time—can transcend the custodial ownership and discretion of a company.

And this is no pipedream either.

Consider the case of 'Axie Infinity.'

This popular play-to-earn environment has, during 2021, advanced from just 4000 users to over 2million and becoming especially popular in countries like the Philippines and Venezuela.

And a big part of why, is that for players in countries like those, the income they can earn inside this digital world is far more significant than what their local physical economy can offer them.

Again, as with the art world, it seems to be a case of decentralization driving democratization.

And this NFT driven revolution and disruption has quickly extended beyond the worlds of gaming and art into the world of music too.

Again, like gaming, music has already seen a decade or more of unprecedented disruption and change, with the arrival of streaming and the likes of Spotify.

However, throughout this wave of disruption, we have seen only a slight shift in power from the publishers and platform owners to the actual artists themselves. The big bad record company has merely transitioned into Spotify, taking all the rewards and the music industry remains heavily centralized.

In financial terms, this translates to an industry that generates roughly $42 billion in revenue but still less than 12% of which goes to the artists themselves.

Similarly, data shows that around 90% of streams on platforms such as Spotify and Apple Music are still from just the top 1% of artists, meaning most artists still get paid fractions of pennies per stream.

Crypto and NFT's, however, look set to change this significantly.

They offer an easy way for artists to mint their work and pull the value directly from their fans, bringing increased decentralization and democracy just as in the traditional art world.

As an example, independent artist, Daniel Allan, who previously only made hundreds of dollars per month from Spotify despite racking up millions of streams, is now making thousands from minting NFTs of his music, according to a recent TIME magazine report.

However, not to be outmaneuvered, the more prominent music publishers are increasingly turning to other areas of the NFT universe to bring innovation.

As a case in point, we recently saw Universal music, one of the biggest publishers, announce the formation of a new supergroup called KINGSHIP, whose members are four bored ape yacht club NFT's.

And we are also seeing the NFT craze applied to historical, cultural phenomenon, long considered dead, for example the Tamagotchi.

Tamagotchi were handheld digital pets, on key chains, which became one of the biggest toy fads of the late 1990s and the early 2000s, selling over 83 million units that have been sold worldwide before seemingly dying out.

But guess what?

They are back, resurrected by the NFT and now called Wamagotchis!

Now while the first Wamagotchi sadly died as it was not fed enough Ethereum currency to keep it alive, in recent months, we have seen the emergence of NFT projects such as METAPETS and MICROPETS, using the same allure of owning and looking after a digital pet which is acquired as an NFT.

And this is an excellent segue into the role of cryptocurrency in all of this.

Because in a world where everything can and increasingly is for sale or purchase as an NFT, you need a scalable mechanism or means to value and transact these items.

And that quite simply is the role of cryptocurrency.

If NFT's are the content, then cryptocurrency is the currency, payment, and value mechanism for this brave new world of digital content.

And this is highly significant because, whether by design or not, the NFT has suddenly given some degree of reason or possible utility to some of the mem coins highlighted previously.

Whether it is launching a full play-to-to, earn NFT gaming metaverses such as is the case with FLOKI INU and its Valhalla plans, or looking to offer just a collection of NFT's as is the case with the similarly named FLOKI ROCKET, suddenly the meme coins have a purpose and a potential offer of utility attached to them.

So then, what is the significance of all this, and what does this GREED cycle mean, especially looking towards the future?

Well, I believe it is this.

If Bitcoin and the GOLD cycle it heralded paved the way for the invention and existence of cryptocurrency. Then the current GREED cycle indicates a shift away from the domain of just the computer geek, the crypto miner, and the move into mainstream mass culture.

Crypto is now cool when it wasn't.

It is now in the mainstream media every day.

Social media platforms are awash, with it every hour, every minute, every second of the day.

On a personal level, those who poked fun at me just 12 months ago for my interest and obsession are suddenly offering to buy me lunch so they can pick my brains, and being a geek feels good again.

Just as with the internet in its early days, a brave few pioneered its use and believed in the change it could and would bring, despite the many voices dismissing it as just a fad.

However, fad or not, it is also clear to me that what we are currently seeing is the creation of a giant bubble around cryptocurrency and NFT's fueled in part by a desire to get rich or good old-fashioned greed.

Now, as to whether we have yet attained peak madness or not, and I would suggest we may still have some way to go in 2022, the one thing that I would not dispute is that this as with all bubbles, the question is not if but when this will burst.

For sure, it will be on par with the dot-com bubble bursting, if not indeed even more dramatic, and lots of people are likely to lose a lot of money.

Now ff I could predict when this would be, I would be a wealthy man, and I certainly am not today.

But the one thing I can say with absolute certainty is that once this happens, and the dust settles, we will see the third and final chapter unfold, that of GOOD and something for which many of the foundations are already being laid in the world of cryptocurrency.

So let us be clear from the start. For me, the question is not if cryptocurrency will change our world, but rather how?

HOPEFULLY, as I will explain a little in the confines of the following pages, it is already starting to do that.

While the greed cycle described previously may have masked some of it today, the process of change or good in my story has already begun and begun at a rapid pace.

Now, when we look at the change or revolution that cryptocurrency and its associated facets will bring, this will be far and wide and in ways, we may not have even yet imagined.

And it will do this through two fundamental and related mechanisms, decentralization and democratization.

As it is built on decentralization (remember the 51% rule), cryptocurrency has the potential to redistribute control and, in so doing, democratize the world around us in ways never possible in the past.

But what does that look like, especially in the real world in which we all currently live, or to put it another way, where to start our good story?

The most obvious and sensible is the impact and change it will further bring to the world of money. It is, after all, called cryptocurrency!

And let's start with a very bold assertion, and that assertion is this.

Five years or ten years from now (now being the end of 2021), Cryptocurrencies could well have replaced traditional FIAT currencies and the Dollar, Pound, Yen, and Euro as the main hedge currencies for most of the world.

Some might say that is not a bold assertion but rather one bordering on madness, especially given the simple fact that these currencies have dominated and dictated the direction of what money means to the world for the latter part of the twentieth century.

But here is the thing.

That is not my prediction nor my deluded desire, far from it.

No, it is a prediction captured by the financial industry giant Delloite in a 2021 survey on the future of cryptocurrency and the blockchain.

For its survey, Deloitte canvassed 1,280 senior executives in a range of industries, including financial services, in 10 locations: Brazil, China, UK, Germany, Hong Kong, Japan, Singapore, South Africa, the US, and United Arab Emirates.

In the resulting research published in August 2021, 76% of those surveyed stated that they expect digital assets will replace government-issued currencies within a decade or at least present a solid alternative to them.

And not only that, but the report concluded that,

 "Participation in the age of digital assets is not an option. It is inevitable. Leaders are left only to decide how to use digital assets and the new global financial service infrastructure to their greatest advantage."

Before highlighting that the main blockage to this happening were security concerns and out-of-date financial infrastructures and systems

But if the above still sounds a little theoretical and hard to conceive in the real world, let's look at what I have termed the South American experiment, something that began in the second half of 2021

For as long as anyone can remember, almost all South American economies and currencies have been tied to the US dollar.

Sometimes referred to as the 'GREAT SIN' by many in the region, it has nonetheless been something that has been seen as essentially inevitable until recently and with no apparent alternative from an economic and monetary perspective.

However, recently, the winds of revolution have been blowing in the region, and step forwards, El Salvador, a country with a well-documented revolutionary past.

Now while the recent history of El Salvador has been far less turbulent than in the late 19th to the mid-20th century, when El Salvador endured chronic political and economic instability characterized by coups, revolts, and a succession of authoritarian rulers that ultimately culminated in the Salvadoran civil war from 1979 to 1992, it has certainly not been one of great economic success either.

Blighted by inflationary pressures and continued economic troubles, for many years, El Salvador's largest source of foreign currency has been remittances sent by Salvadoreans abroad, estimated at over $2 billion and delivered by over 2 million Salvadorans living abroad in countries including the United States, Canada, Mexico, Guatemala, Costa Rica, Australia, and Sweden, the great sin as it is called has offered option to escape this adverse situation.

However, something exciting and significant happened in September 2021.

The El Salvador government passed legislation that officially recognized bitcoin as legal tender.

That means you can walk into a McDonald's in El Salvador and buy a burger with Bitcoin if you so desire, and likewise use it to purchase any other goods and services you require, or for that matter, desire.

But while that, I would venture, is very significant in itself, it is the associated and proactive actions of the government alongside this that comprise the actual experiment.

Despite warnings from the INF not to do so, the Salvadoran government led by President Nayib Bukele has decided to go all-in on Bitcoin as an alternative to the great sin and the US Dollar.

This has included the purchase of Bitcoin, with the total holding being around 1391, including a recent purchase of 21 bitcoin on December 21, which president Bukele took to Twitter to announce by tweeting,

"El Salvador's total size is 21,000 km2. Coincidence? I don't think so!"

He then followed it up with further tweets that collectively read:

"Today is the last 21st day of the year 21 of the 21st century. At 21:00 hours, we are buying 21 bitcoins for the occasion!"

And not only that.

Previously in November 2021 president, Bukele had already announced plans to build a Bitcoin city at the base of a volcano, with the cryptocurrency used to fund the project its president has announced.

Circular in shape, to represent a large coin, the intention is to build it in the south-eastern region of La Unión and take advantage of the Conchagua volcano's geothermal energy to power Bitcoin mining.

Yes, that's correct, using Volcanoes to mine bitcoin.

Whether you consider that smart or just plain crazy, what isn't crazy is how they have recognized the democratization potential that comes with cryptocurrency.

As well as cheerleading the government efforts and initiatives around bitcoin, the other significant action taken was to offer the wider population their own individual cryptocurrency wallet, called CHIVO, with initial funding from the Salvadoran government of the equivalent of $30 in bitcoin that could be used for shopping or to pay taxes.

In my view, intelligent recognition of the democratization, if not the decentralization benefits cryptocurrency can bring, but beyond this, the obvious question is, has this experiment worked?

As you would expect, especially from a nation with a somewhat chequered past in realizing democracy and positive social change, the results can certainly not be considered definitive yet, and indeed not anything yet utopian.

Indeed, it has been reported by hundreds of citizens that stores haven't received their payments and that funds have disappeared from their accounts. While following the announcement of bitcoin city, the International Monetary Fund (IMF) repeated its advice that El Salvador stops using Bitcoin as legal tender, pointing to financial and consumer risks associated with the cryptocurrency.

Yet these issues aside, there are two pieces of evidence now in existence which I believe point to the fact that this experiment might well actually be working.

First up is this.

Historically, only around 27 percent of Salvadorans have ever held bank accounts, with most of the population being unbanked' i.e., without access to traditional bank accounts and banking infrastructure instead of relying on cash or barter to transact.

Now while that alone, given the history and current economic position of El Salvador, may not seem shocking, when you consider that currently, 47 percent of the same population now hold cryptocurrency wallets in the form of the government supplied Chivo version, up from zero in August 2021, it rapidly becomes so.

Secondly, and equally intriguing, in my opinion, is a second fact on the value of that holding.

The inflation rate in El Salvador is currently at around 6.2 percent year-on-year as of November 2021, meaning in simplistic terms that any local currency held buys them 6.2 percent less in real terms.

However, for those holding cryptocurrency in their Chivo wallets, the spending power of that holding has risen by 30 percent between September and November 2021, driven by the increase in the value of bitcoin.

Now, of course, these two facts alone, especially the latter, which comes with a considerable number of caveats, are not proof of success.

But regardless, what is occurring in El Salvador points to the enormous potential for change that cryptocurrency can potentially bring both in social and economic terms.

Whether bitcoin can indeed deliver El Salvador liberation from the great sin of the dollar remains to be seen.

Still, regardless, they are already being joined by other South American neighbors in attempting to do so.

Venezuela is another case in point.

Like El Salvador, Venezuela has had a troubled and turbulent history since its independence in 1830.

As anyone versed in the geography and politics of the region knows, Venezuela has the world's largest known oil reserves. It has also been one of the leading exporters of oil in the twentieth century.

Yet despite this vast natural wealth, it very much remains a developing country and only ranks 113th on the human development index.

As a result of the excesses and poor policies of the incumbent government, the country's economy constantly teeters on the brink of collapse and struggles with record hyperinflation, unemployment, and poverty.

As early as 2017, Venezuela was already declared to be in default regarding its global debt payments by the US and international credit rating agencies, meaning that by 2020 more than three million people had fled the country due to the economic situation.

But recently, this total basket case of a country, seemingly without any real hope of change or escaping its economic woes and hyperinflation, has, like its neighbor El Salvador turned to cryptocurrency as a possible solution and means of escape from its dependence on the US dollar and the great sin of doing so.

As hyperinflation and US sanctions disrupt Venezuela's economy, cryptocurrency has rapidly emerged to provide services that usually would be handled by the traditional banking system.

But unlike El Salvador, there is not a single solution. Instead, we are seeing two different approaches emerging.

On the official government side, the petro (₽), or petromoneda, was launched in February 2018 as the official government-backed cryptocurrency of Venezuela.

This was intended to supplement Venezuela's plummeting bolivar Fuerte ('strong Bolívar') currency and circumvent US sanctions and improve access to international financing, given the country's poor credit status.

To further support this, in August of that year, they also launched the sovereign Bolívar, with the government stating it would be linked to the petro coin value. However, they had already created petro gold in February of that year, with the same objective in mind.

Now, as the above hints at, this government-backed attempt at moving to cryptocurrency had a far from the promising start, with its launch and subsequent deployment at best being chaotic, and at worst, a total disaster.

What more the US department of the treasuring warned that participating in the petro cryptocurrency could violate US sanctions as it "would appear to be an extension of credit to the Venezuelan government," and Trump signed an order prohibiting transactions by a United States person or within the United States to this effect.

Yet despite this inauspicious start, President Maduro continued to push the Petro.

Presumably, with the intent of boosting the currency's utilization in a 2020 speech to the Constituent Assembly, he announced that airlines flying from Caracas would be required to pay for fuel in Petros.

Now it does not require a degree in rocket science to realize that the Petro is ultimately doomed to failure.

Conceived by the president to circumvent international sanctions against his regime and revive the country's flailing economy, any hope of being considered an actual cryptocurrency vanished recently when the Petro ledger was shut down for "maintenance"— impossible on an existing blockchain.

At the same time, mining nodes must be registered with the Venezuelan government, again invalidating the decentralized requirement.

So, if the Petro is not an actual cryptocurrency, and from the current evidence, a total failure, then why reference it here?

Well, because all the activity and publicity around it has woken its population up to the potential of real cryptocurrency to bring the change that Venezuela so badly needs.

Recently, Reuters reported that food delivery driver Pablo Toro as evidence of this.

Now while he has no investment in cryptocurrency or blockchain, Pablo uses digital tokens every time he sends money to his family from neighboring Colombia, where he works.

Using an app called Valiu to receive Colombian pesos, he then uses those to buy cryptocurrency that he sells on LocalBitcoins, a global peer-to-peer (or DeFi) site for trading tokens in local currencies.

While far from simple, for Pablo and many other Venezuelan migrants, cryptocurrency has rapidly become the main channel to send money home.

And as hyperinflation and US sanctions disrupt Venezuela's economy, cryptocurrency is rapidly emerging as a means to access and move money for the wider population both within the country and beyond.

And this is also true of Migrants from another south American country, Cuba.

Many Cubans working abroad have now turned to cryptocurrency to send money back to Cuba in recent months.

Sending and receiving money between the US and Cuba had become became extremely difficult under the Trump administration.

In 2020, Western Union, a particularly effective channel for doing so, shuttered all its 400-plus locations amid increasingly aggressive Trump-era sanctions.

And given the process of getting money into and out of the country was made even more complicated by the Covid-19 pandemic, it is not hard to work out why, in the latter half of 2021, the Cuban government, noted for being highly conservative in a Marxist kind of way, announced it would officially recognize and attempt to regulate cryptocurrency.

And this crypto experiment continues to spread and scale across the entire Latam region.

Recently Brazil, South America's most populated country and largest economy, indicated that it is looking to join El Salvador and make Bitcoin legal tender. Rumors abound of other South American countries considering following suit.

So now armed with this evidence in hand, let's reconsider the Delloite report and its assertion that in 5-120 years could see the replacement of traditional FIAT currencies by cryptocurrencies.

I would venture this looks far from a crazy pipe dream or prediction for the Latam region, but more like the actual direction of travel.

And alongside the various geopolitical and social factors driving this adoption, there is also another critical factor: mobility.

While access to traditional banking infrastructures and even identity remains impossible for many, access to mobile devices and 3G or greater is within reach of the majority.

Smartphone connections in Latin America have reached 500 million by the end of 2021 – or 74% of the population. Compare that, if you will to the average access to bank accounts at 54%, and the opportunity to jump straight to cryptocurrency becomes apparent.

And if this factor is also a key driver in the Latam move to cryptocurrency adoption, be it one with clearly many bumps in the road to come, then it is likely to be an even more significant driver in that other great sub-continent, Africa.

According to globaleconomy.com, average bank account penetration in Africa remains low at 32%, and in some countries such as Chad, it even sits in single figures.

Access to traditional banking and money services and the crucial identity requirement remains extremely low throughout the region, especially in the sub-Saharan areas.

This means that Africa is the continent of the unbanked and the most significant component of some two billion individuals globally, according to McKinsey, who lack access to formal savings and credit.

Contrast this to mobile phone access, which sits at around 46% or 495million persons and is estimated to rise to 615million by 2025.

It is entirely accurate that more people now have access to mobile devices than electricity in some sub-Saharan countries, raising the obvious question of how they then charge their devices.

But that challenge aside, as with the Latam region, the opportunity to move straight to cryptocurrency is evident.

Already the proliferation of money sending apps in the region is enormous, apps that offer "mobile money" via digital payments, where no bank account is required to facilitate the transaction as the telecom provider performs this function instead.

Indeed, according to the Wall Street Journal, "nearly half of the 1.04 billion registered mobile money accounts worldwide are in sub-Saharan.

Africa, while Mckinsey notes that over half of the 282 mobile money services operating worldwide are in the region.

As a case in point, while only 11% of Ugandans have a bank account, 43% already use a mobile payment account, meaning that it is quite a small step to go from a fiat-based peer-to-peer platform to one based on the blockchain and crypto.

Against this backdrop, it is no surprise that the cryptocurrency revolution finds many willing advocates in the region, the second-most-populous globally.

The world economic forum recently noted that during 2021, the cryptocurrency market in the region grew by a stunning $105.6billion.

And this is even more staggering when you factor in that most African regimes and central banks are hostile to cryptocurrency exchanges.

For example, the Central Bank of Nigeria (CBN) has banned all banks since 2017 from using, holding, trading, and transacting in cryptocurrencies.

But for many of the population, cryptocurrencies offer a new alternative, and an escape, just as in Latam, from the perils of broken economies and high inflation with the resultant devaluation of their fiat currencies.

And to further prove the point, taking the Nigerian Naira (NGN) as an example, since 2017 and the crypto ban, its value has dropped by nearly 52% since the central bank banned cryptocurrency activities.

In comparison, bitcoin has gained over 11,000% in value during the same time frame.

And this stance by central governments has had another, perhaps unintended consequence too, accelerating the move away from big exchanges such as Binance to smaller peer-to-peer ones such as Paxful and Remitano.

A significant number of transactions are also taking place over informal messaging apps rather than on conventional platforms DeFi platforms.

Adedeji Owonibi, the founder of Nigerian blockchain consultancy company Convexity, recently commented on this when he said, "Informal P2P trading is huge in Nigeria on WhatsApp and Telegram. I've seen young people and businessmen in these groups carry out transactions for several million with popular OTC merchants."

And while at present the official stance of many governments in the region is an anti-cryptocurrency one, perhaps intrigued by the south American experiments, many are nonetheless now looking to launch their own virtual money, backed and issued by central banks.

And given its expansionist policies, already in evidence for many years in that region, it will come as no surprise that many of these plans include the involvement of the Chinese state, which is an excellent segue into that other great continent, Asia.

So let us start with China.

Now again, it does not take a rocket science degree to work out that the two fundamental principles underpinning the cryptocurrency revolution, decentralization, and democratization, are about as far removed from the ethos of the Chinese communist government as you can get.

And as if to highlight this further, China's Central Bank has again stressed that all transactions of crypto currencies are illegal, stating

"Virtual currency-related business activities are illegal financial activities,"

the People's Bank of China said, warning it

"Seriously endangers the safety of people's assets."

And it seems this position is being enforced too. Until recently, China accounted for 75% of all bitcoin mining activity, with its relatively low electricity costs and cheaper computer hardware, but this has now fallen back to around 46% and is in decline due to this overt anti-mining policy the government.

Similarly, Binance, currently the world's largest cryptocurrency exchange, moved its operations out of China, where Changpeng Zhao founded it, and into the Cayman Islands in 2018 due to government regulation and restrictions.

Yes, despite all its official rhetoric and this constant 'banning' of cryptocurrency and crypto mining, it would be fair to say that the Chinese regime recognizes the already colossal potential and impact that cryptocurrency can have on itself and, importantly, beyond its borders.

And if that were not the case, then why would China and its government currently be the second holder of Bitcoin globally?

And yes, that fact is 100 percent true when writing this.

And while trading cryptocurrency has officially been banned in China since 2019, many of its population have continued doing this online through foreign exchanges via VPN, something that the government is aware of.

So, what exactly then is going on with China and cryptocurrency?

Well, the conspiracy theorists in the world of crypto, and it does seem to attract many such individuals, would point to the fact that all of this is part of a carefully choreographed master plan to destabilize the west and its democracies.

Now, of course, this may have some validity, certainly considering the current stake that China's government has in bitcoin; I am not convinced that it is as well-conceived as plan as this theory suggests.

And while that is not to say that they could indeed be using the world of blockchain for non-good purposes, and to be fair, they seem to have an existing form for such behavior in recent years through cyber hacking; I think it is more likely to result from their aspirations for the digital Yuan, a cryptocurrency designed for the authoritarian state.

Now initially in line with its quest to be an advanced economy, China originally appeared to embrace cryptocurrency and opened its first bitcoin exchange in 2011, and by 2016 was a profoundly influential player in the industry.

But since 2012, when Xi Jinping took over leadership of China, that crypto calculus has changed.

Quite simply, as indicated earlier, the essence of cryptocurrencies as decentralized tender that can help democratize influence and power is deeply at odds with the Chinese Communist Party's governing approach under Xi, and any privately developed digital currency will always be a threat to the central bank authority.

Therefore, after some eight years of development, the digital Yuan was unveiled in 2020.

Distributed to consumers by the central bank via six major commercial banks, usually through a wallet app, users can make payments by scanning QR codes or using wearable devices, including physical wallets embedded with digital yuan chips.

It also incorporates a simple yet brilliant feature that will make it more attractive, especially amongst China's massive rural population.

And that is that people can transact with it even if they're not connected to the internet, simply by tapping two digital-yuan-enabled phones together.

And alongside this, Huawei has also started shipping their smartphones preinstalled with a digital yuan wallet.

So then, how is the rollout of the world's authoritarian cryptocurrency going?

Well, according to the Chinese government, so apply a generous pinch of salt; by June 2021, there were around 20million digital yuan wallets with a transaction volume of 34.5 billion Yuan ($5.3 billion).

And while that might sound impressive, especially when you consider only around 200million crypto wallets worldwide as we head towards the end of 2021, bearing in mind that China has a population of 1.4billion, it would be fair to say it still has some way to go.

But it seems China is determined to unleash its digital Yuan onto the world stage. Next year, the Beijing Winter Olympics will feature ATMs that can convert foreign currencies, including US dollars, into Chinese virtual money, carried in a digital yuan wallet card.

Now as to whether we will all be using digital Yuan in five years, I am not so sure, and while the Chinese government's unswerving belief in the digital Yuan is impressive, I, for one, very much doubt it will stand the test of time, not least because In China, an enormous share of digital payments is already being handled by private-sector mobile wallets like Alipay and WeChat Pay, meaning that any such move can easily be compared as a regression to the government food stamps of the past, which indeed many are already saying.

But while China seems determined to reinvent cryptocurrencies to their rules, the adoption of existing cryptos is gaining pace across the rest of the continent.

Crypto-related activity in the fast-growing economies across the Asia-Pacific region increased by 706% between July 2020 and June 2021, according to blockchain analytics company Chainalysis.

That translates into $572.5 billion or 14% of total global transaction value in dollar terms, and of that, a significant percentage went through DeFi platforms.

Again, as in Latam, existing familiarity with money apps, mobile use, and the fact that centralized exchanges in many countries such as India are becoming more problematic if not impossible to use means that crypto adoption for the mass population is increasingly happening through decentralized peer to peer platforms away from Government control and regulation.

And this is one of the key reasons why, when we look at the biggest adopters of cryptocurrency in the region, we find Vietnam right up there with the likes of India, with an astonishing 42 percent of the population investing in cryptocurrency and 28 percent holding bitcoin.

Allied to a long history of distrust in the Vietnamese Dong, which has a tradition of losing value quickly, and a resultant desire to look for assets that hold value more securely than cash, this means that the Vietnamese have been at the forefront of cryptocurrency adoption.

Turning our attention to India, we find a fast-growing market, one where cryptocurrency is increasingly gaining prominence as a payment method among businesses in India's formal and informal economy.

Again, we find essential factors that can help drive adoption, including a straight-to-mobile population.

And while, as a result of efforts by the Narendra Modi government in previous years to give banking access all, 80% of the population of 1.38billion, in theory, have a bank account, for many mistrusts of traditional banking, means many do not utilize this route.

However, while this would indicate India, not least given its population size as a likely leader in cryptocurrency heading forwards, just as in China, the Indian government is preparing to ban private cryptocurrencies and allow the country's central bank to launch an official digital currency.

Flagged in a parliamentary bulletin listing upcoming legislation, The Cryptocurrency and Regulation of Official Digital Currency Bill aims to

"Create a facilitative framework for the creation of the official digital currency to be issued by the Reserve Bank of India,"

However, it adds,

"The bill also seeks to prohibit all private cryptocurrencies in India."

It is evident then that although considered a democracy, unlike China, India fears the potential impacts that cryptocurrency for the mass could have on its economic and social influence, although Prime minister, Narendra Modi, suggested its concern was that they would "spoil our youth," whatever that means.

And closer to home, or at least where I reside in the western world, we find growing noise about regulation and restrictions as cryptocurrency awareness and adoption start to reach a more critical mass.

In the United States, the Biden administration has recently outlined legislation to bring more regulation to the cryptocurrency market.

And in recent months, US Federal Reserve Chairman Jerome Powell and Security and Exchange Commission (SEC) Chairman Gary Gensler have expressed concern over the lack of regulation while pursuing Ripple labs and its XRP currency through the courts.

And whether they have a valid case or not, it is a clear signal of intent regardless.

While in the United Kingdom, the Bank of England recently told the BBC that "Fast-growing crypto-currency assets could pose a danger to the established financial system, and that the bank needed to be ready to contain those risks."

However, it also talks up the potential of a digital pound, which sounds very familiar, doesn't it!

And the reason that sounds familiar is that whether it is China, El Salvador, or the United States, cryptocurrency is starting to deliver on its first potential for good by decentralizing financial control and, as a result, increasing the potential for more democratization of power and influence.

Whether an authoritarian regime, such as in China or a mature western democracy such as the United Kingdom, the impact of this decentralization and democratization means the same thing, and that is a decline in control and influence of government and central banks, again taking us back to the Deloitte predictions around FIAT currency erosion.

Then factor in the challenges and potential tax impacts of moving away from sovereign currencies and towards a digital currency that doesn't recognize such borders and restrictions. Unsurprisingly, no government is a fan or advocate of the cryptocurrency revolution, although ultimately, this is, in my opinion, a revolution they cannot resist.

However, it would be a huge mistake to believe that cryptocurrency and the associated blockchain technologies will bring change only in the financial world.

Yes, of course, it is a critical part of their design, intent, and allure, to decentralize and democratize the control of financial wealth and power away from just a few and towards the many.

But cryptocurrency can and will extend its impact well beyond just the financial world, and in my view, will change the wider world too.

And a lot of this change will, and to some extent already is, start to deliver on the promise of cryptocurrency as an agent of good and positive change in the world.

And once you start to look at ways in which cryptocurrency is already being used outside of the financial systems to drive revolution and change, you rapidly realize that sky is the limit, or perhaps that should be our imagination.

So, with that in mind, let's look at some of the areas in which cryptocurrency starts impacting and delivering on its potential for good.

The global supply chain is one of the most significant areas that cryptocurrency and the blockchain are starting to revolutionize is the worldwide supply chain.

One great example is Vechain (VET).

This cryptocurrency focuses specifically on the B2B and supply chain space and application and enhances supply chain management and business processes.

Built on a bespoke enterprise blockchain platform and consisting of two distinct cryptocurrency tokens, Vechain (VET) and VeChainThor Energy (VTHO), (The former is used to transfer value across VeChains network, and the latter is used as energy or "gas" to power transactions),

its goal is to streamline these processes and information flow for complex supply chains.

Somewhat unique, the two-token system was devised for effective governance and a predictable economic model and to enable a balance between decentralized benefits and the centralized needs of global business.

Now granted, at first, that may not sound very exciting or revolutionary, but once we start to look at the existing real-world applications of this cryptocurrency, it certainly does deliver on both counts.

Now, unless you have been living on Mars for the last few years, you will not have failed to notice the growing and serious problem of plastic pollution in the world's oceans.

While many initiatives are now established to address this issue, one of note on a global scale is the ReSea project.

ReSea Project is a Danish organization focused on cleaning up the oceans by removing plastics and recycling them while raising awareness of proper waste disposal.

Initially concentrating its efforts on the North Sea, it now serves most oceanic regions, and one of the innovative ways it has approached this is by partnering with Vechain.

ReSea adopts a community-driven approach, meaning that people in local communities are employed to recover the plastic polluting oceans and rivers and deliver this to designated waste banks.

VeChain and an associated mobile App collect, record, and monitor data at the identified critical control points of the collection process.

Vechain is used to record and verify the plastic extraction and quantities, which helps ensure fair compensation to the local collection cleanup team and identify elements of the global supply chain that may contribute to the waste plastic itself.

Now I cannot do justice in the confines of this book to just how powerful this partnership is becoming, nor how much it acts as a poster child for the good that cryptocurrency can bring to the world, so I would very much advocate taking time to Google ReSea and find out more.

At this stage, it is also worth briefly mentioning the cryptocurrency, Alogrand ALGO.

One of the new blockchains that use a pure proof of stake model, on April 22, 2021, Algorand announced that its blockchain had become carbon neutral and intends to become carbon negative soon.

It is also looking to establish itself as a critical player in sustainable energy technology. For example, it is currently partnering with a Spanish financial technology firm, ClimateTrade, to create a CO_2 marketplace for industries.

And turning back to VeChain, ReSea is just one example of how cryptocurrency is being used to revolutionize the world of supply chains and bring good to bear through decentralization of these.

And VeChain has inked numerous partnerships in recent months to this end.

From a partnership with Italian pasta Producer De Cecco to validate the integrity of its global supply chain partners through to a partnership with Renault and Microsoft to create a digital car maintenance book that cannot be tampered with, VeChain stands as hard proof of how cryptocurrency is already changing global business for good.

And seeing as we have just mentioned automotive, it is worth highlighting that Porsche's Panamera is the first blockchain-enabled car.

According to Claudio Weck, blockchain and AI architect at Porsche, this gives the customer security and secure sharing of vehicle data between the owner and people. They may need to interact with the car, such as mechanics.

Additionally, he highlights the benefit regarding the product life cycle and that a blockchain-enabled car can never have its mileage tampered with,

before then highlighting the convenience of recording historical vehicle data, including payments, in this manner.

And while we are talking about luxury items, and I think it is fair to describe a Porsche as such, cryptocurrency is also bringing good to bear for purchasers of such items by tackling the age-old problem of Fraud.

At a conservative estimate, the value of high-end goods sold in the counterfeit market is around $98 billion in just one year.

Luxury brands spend millions a year in legal fees alone to fight counterfeiters. At the same time, the negative impact on consumers is much harder to quantify but likely to be significantly higher still.

Cryptocurrency and its associated decentralized blockchain technology offer an almost perfect solution to this problem.

Items can quickly be recorded and, more importantly, authenticated on a decentralized ledger, and as with the Porsche example above, their history is transparent to all.

As a realization of this promise, in 2021, we have seen LVMH, Richemont, and the Prada Group forming a non-profit alliance known as the Aura Blockchain Consortium.

By embedding chips in handbags and serial numbers for watches and fine jewelry, they are moving away from old methods such as certificates of authenticity, which were open to Fraud.

And that other stalwart of the luxury item, Chanel, will implant small square plaques with the CC logo with an embedded serial code accessible only by utilizing blockchain technology to verify its authenticity, allowing them to record each of their bags and move away from the carte authenticate, which has long been open to abuse.

But it is not just in the luxury world where this cryptocurrency application will be transformational.

Indeed, while it may be hard to argue that removing Fraud from luxury goods is really doing good, doing so from items that can have a direct and highly negative effect on people's well-being and even live certainly can.

Cryptocurrency can and already is being used to address the problem of fake medication. Currently worth a staggering $200 annually, the Counterfeit Drug Market has grown by 20% year on year. Even more alarmingly, that is twice the rate of the legitimate pharmaceutical market and accounts for 2.5% of the total global pharma market.

Deploying cryptocurrency technology can help reduce the over 1 million deaths annually, according to the World Health Organization, resulting from counterfeit and substandard drugs.

And cryptocurrency and blockchain technology is even being used to ensure that legitimate medicines are being administered correctly.

CNBC recently reported how two hospitals in the UK are actively using blockchain technology to help maintain the temperature of coronavirus vaccines before administering them to patients.

Using the Hedera cryptocurrency and blockchain, a consortium backed by both IBM and Google, the objective is to keep a tamper-proof digital record of temperature-sensitive vaccines, meaning that they would spot any irregularities in the storage of the vaccines before administering them to patients.

And moving on from the world of medicine to that of transportation, while none of us would, I am sure, knowingly get on an airplane repaired with fake or substandard parts, the sad truth is that several air disasters have resulted because historically, the $45billion aircraft parts industry has been open to such problems.

As a case in point, on September 8, 1989, at 22,000 feet over the North Sea, the tail section of a Convair 580 turboprop plane began vibrating violently and tore loose due to unregulated and defective parts being used in maintenance, and tragically resulting in the death of all 55 people on board.

And in the world of automotive, it is estimated that around 36,000 persons die each year resulting from accidents caused by defective or fake parts.

Again, here the application of crypto technology here helps remove and mitigate this risk.

As indicated in the earlier Porsche example, every part of the machine, from engines to tiny bolts, can, in theory, be verified and checked in near real-time against a decentralized ledger.

And these are just but a few examples of where cryptocurrency and its associated technology platforms are already bringing good to bear in our modern world.

And while such good benefits for consumers may be hidden or a little less obvious, we also see the positive impact of the cryptocurrency revolution in our more overt interactions with the modern world as consumers.

One such area is retailing and associated customer loyalty schemes.

Still adjusting, it seems, to the wave of change brought by e-commerce and accelerated by the recent COVID pandemic, the world of retail is now bracing itself for a further revolution to be initiated by cryptocurrency.

Now while one might assume this is yet to get going, and to be fair, unless you happen to be buying a burger in El Salvador, using cryptocurrency to make purchases is still not an everyday occurrence, it would be unwise not to recognize the proximity to this being the case.

As proof of this, in December of 2021, Visa's head of cryptocurrency, Cuy Sheffield, revealed that the payments giant has already partnered with about 60 leading cryptocurrencies and platforms to make it easy for consumers to convert and spend digital currency at 80 million merchants worldwide.

And yes, that is correct, 80million merchants worldwide.

Similarly, Mastercard announced in late October 2021 that any of the thousands of banks and millions of merchants on its payments network would soon be able to integrate crypto into its products.

To do this, it will partner with crypto company Bakkt and include bitcoin wallets, credit and debit cards that earn rewards in crypto, and loyalty programs offered in cryptocurrency.

And while some of this has yet to be realized into 2022 and beyond, the list of retailers where you can already use cryptocurrencies may surprise you.

For example, travel giant Expedia is one of the most prominent travel agencies to accept Bitcoin through its partnership with Travala, meaning you can now book 700,000 hotels using more than 30 different cryptos, including Bitcoin.

And getting there shouldn't be a problem either with airlines also getting in on the act.

Latvian airline Air Baltic has accepted bitcoin as payment for fares back in 2014 and was followed shortly after by LOT Polish Airlines, while more recently, in September 2021, Universal Air Travel Plan (UATP,) an airline-owned global payment network with more than 300 airline members and travel merchants, including Air Canada, Air China, Delta, Frontier, Japan Airlines, Jetblue, Qantas, Southwest, and United confirmed that it would now accept payment in cryptocurrency too, including Dogecoin.

And given that airlines are known for their loyalty schemes, that seems like a nice segue into crypto's impact on those.

For so long, stuck in what sometimes seems like a time warp, customer loyalty has seemed to do the opposite and restrict consumers' benefits by restricting them to a specific purveyor of goods or services if they were to see any actual use from such schemes.

So perhaps unsurprisingly, we are seeing the world of cryptocurrency collide with customer loyalty schemes and CRM with some vigor.

And this collision takes one of two forms.

The first model, and perhaps most apparent, is rewarding purchases with cryptocurrency that they can then either use or exchange for others or FIAT currencies.

For example, I now hold a crypto.com VISA card that rewards me in CRO for any retail purchases, leaving me free to convert that into either other cryptocurrencies or FIAT money.

And I am not alone.

VISA, the world's largest debit and credit card issuer, was reported by Forbes magazine to have facilitated more than $1 billion in transactions via crypto-linked Visa cards in the first half of 2021 alone.

And around the world are starting to see many other retailers embrace the idea of cryptocurrency-based reward schemes.

From the Dubai mall, where you can earn and spend rewards in cryptocurrency, to Grand Reserve, a rewards points operator for wine lovers; consumers are increasingly interested in receiving cryptocurrency rewards, with 44% of Americans indicating they are interested in receiving digital currencies as an alternative to traditional cash-back reward programs in a recent survey by coruzant.com.

And not only does this increase the good for consumers, but it also benefits the provider, allowing the companies to record what their customers are consuming, when, in what quantity, and with what frequency.

The second way in which cryptocurrency looks set to revolutionize customer loyalty schemes is through what is known as the airdrop.

Not to be confused with the apple-based technology, in the world of cryptocurrency, consumers are airdropped or gifted cryptocurrency tokens or even NFT's via their public cryptocurrency keys or addresses.

TO facilitate this, those doing the airdrop take a snapshot of individuals holding a specific cryptocurrency or NFT from the publicly available ledger or blockchain and then share this out to those individuals based on apparent criteria such as volume of tokens held.

Increasingly becoming a big thing, especially around the world of NFTs, airdrops hint at the future of not just retail loyalty schemes but also those for cryptocurrency too, with the recent sologenic (SOLO) airdrop to XRP crypto holders being an excellent example of this being used to increase value around a specific cryptocurrency.

If you are interested in finding out what airdrops are happening and don't want to spend hours trawling the internet, look at www.airdrop.io, which provides an excellent overview in one location, or at least did at the time of writing.

And the airdrop is also a critical component of what I believe is the biggest driver of change or good that the world of cryptocurrency is helping bring, and that is the transition to what many call the metaverse, but which the more enlightened have recently started to rename WEB3.

I touched on the metaverse earlier, and it is a critical component in the migration of cryptocurrency from greed to good. Still, there are a few problems with describing what is happening as just the metaverse, because for me, it is something much more comprehensive, of which a metaverse is just a part.

And the recent cynical, and yes, I use that word on purpose, move by Facebook to rename itself meta, and both attempt to landgrab while diverting attention away from the fact that it was voted the worst company of 2021 by a recent Yahoo! audience poll, has done little to help matters.

So, for absolute clarity, Facebook is certainly not the metaverse and never will be, and the metaverse is not the entirety of WEB3 and likewise never will be.

Web3, internet3, or whatever new words we find to describe it, is a complete reinvention of the internet from top to bottom.

And web3 is entirely based on the founding principles of cryptocurrency, those being decentralization and democratization.

If web1 was about introducing the internet to our lives, and web2 was about mobile and the emergence of what is sometimes called the platform age, where technology and big data, with centralized control and influence of that data dominated by the significant few, web3 is the opposite.

Web3, already in construction, is based on the new decentralized technology of the blockchain, where competition and control infrastructure must give way to consensus and collaboration, and the voice of the many will determine the future direction, not the vanity of the few.

It also brings a new mindset, where technology and data become subservient to creativity, and the philosophy is one of let's create.

And what will be created is limited by what we can imagine. As indicated earlier, the evidence already exists and is growing by the day, of the change and ultimately good that this new world can bring to everyone on the planet.

Now, of course, this is a very ideological perspective, perhaps even a utopia in outlook.

After many years involved in the world of technology and the internet, both personally and professionally, I am not naive enough to think that only good will come from this change, nor that everything promised will be realized.

As I have already covered earlier in this book, it has already brought a lot of negatives that play to our worst human behaviors, greed central amongst them.

But that aside, I believe that Web3 offers a new beginning and a chance for the internet, one of man's greatest inventions, to at last realize its real potential for good.

So, with my anti-platform rant and utopian soapbox preaching over, what does this have to do with cryptocurrency?

Well, this.

If we accept that web3 is built on the blockchain, enabled and delivered by technology including AR (augmented reality) and VR (virtual reality), populated by NFT's as the content and creativity within. In that case, cryptocurrency can be considered its currency and capital.

Or, to put it another way.

Cryptocurrency is the lifeblood of web3.

Simple as that.

Not only has it rapidly started to become the currency used to transact within this brave new world, but it is also now becoming the source of capital to build and expand it.

Again, if we accept for a moment that web1 was funded by venture capital, web2 was supplemented by crowding funding through the likes of kickstarter.com, then web3 is going to be primarily funded by the issuing cryptocurrency as its capital source.

In recent months, the massive flurry of new cryptocurrencies emerging has seen a shift away from just the meme coins or tokens referenced earlier, with no apparent value or utility, to currencies primarily designed to fund the future growth of web3, in particular, the metaverse component.

For the first time in the development of the internet, we are seeing its future development and control transfer away from just the haves to now and includes the have not's.

Yes, of course, big finance and venture capital play a significant role in all of this. In fact, during 2021, some $30billion flowed into the development of web3 from such sources, but the critical difference is that now big corporations or even venture capitalists are not needed to fund the next big thing.

All that is needed is creativity, vision, and some code to deliver the next big thing, as decentralization starts to give digital democracy to the many.

So, if that all sounds exciting, be it still a little utopia, the obvious question then becomes one of what next and how quickly this world of web3 become our reality.

Now while my credentials as a futurologist are somewhat limited, not least as I questioned the purpose of many key drivers in web2 when they first emerged.

However, I will nonetheless now fire up the DeLorean and give you my perspective on what I think will play out in the next few years as the cryptocurrency revolution continues to gain momentum.

The problem with futurology is that it tends not to age well, especially when I am involved.

But regardless, in my opinion, as we head out of 2021 and into 2022, and let's hope it is a better year than the previous two, I believe we are only just starting to see the true potential of the cryptocurrency and its impact on our daily lives.

I genuinely believe that five years from now, if not sooner, we will look back and realize quite what a monumental revolution the cryptocurrency one was and do so from a world fundamentally different from the one in which I write this today.

Now, of course, time will tell if my futurology powers have improved since my earlier efforts around web1 and web2.

And my bullish outlook is based on several factors, which, regardless of your opinion on whether cryptocurrency is a good or bad thing, cannot be ignored.

Firstly, while we are still at the early stage of consumer adoption, with a mere 200 million people worldwide actively engaged in using cryptocurrency in 2021, the adoption curve closely matches that drawn for the internet itself.

And even if it merely continues to follow that trajectory and not surpass it as many are predicting, that means that in a mere ten years, we will have over $4billion people using cryptocurrency.

And even with just that user base of 200million, the cryptocurrency space already has a market value somewhere in the region of $3trillion.

And using some admittedly elementary math's means that cryptocurrency could have a value above $60trillion in ten years.

And while many point to a lack of regulation and the current hostile rhetoric from many governments, where, according to a 2021 report by the US Law Library of Congress, a total of 51 countries in the world have currently imposed bans of some kind on cryptocurrencies, as significant risks and red flags, what they do not highlight is this.

And that is that some 79 nations, including many who have attempted to ban cryptocurrency in the short term, are actively researching, developing, piloting, or launching their own central bank digital currencies.

For me, this points to one obvious outcome.

And that is simply is that increasingly, all the world's governments and financial gatekeepers recognize that the cryptocurrency revolution, started by bitcoin back in 2010, cannot be halted or reversed.

As such, they are looking to find ways of accepting cryptocurrency on their own terms, as central bank digital currencies (or CBDC's for short) digital versions of government-issued money.

Like Bitcoin, they can be used for fast and inexpensive global payments. Still, unlike Bitcoin, CBDCs are centralized legal tender, created and controlled by a government or central bank.

As such, they do not, in my view, represent an accurate representation of cryptocurrency if the base principles of decentralization and democracy or consensus are to be followed. I expect them to have limited success and take up compared to their truly decentralized peers.

But regardless of the outcome, and the forthcoming digital Yuan experiment around the Olympics will doubtless be fascinating, once a government has fully unleashed the cryptocurrency genie from the bottle, be it a bottle they have created, there will be no going back.

Another reason I am very bullish about the future of cryptocurrency is quite simply because the monetary system is broken and needs the upgrade that crypto brings.

It was never designed to support the internet, e-commerce, and a globalized cross-border economy.

And don't be fooled by that shiny banking app on your smartphone, either. Behind it lie computer systems developed in the '70s and '80s and programmed in languages like cobalt.

When cryptocurrency can move millions, billions, or even trillions of dollars in seconds and for a few cents in fees, why would anyone not want to move to adopt that.

And one of my favorite anecdotes from 2021 tells how a billion dollars' worth of bitcoin was moved in a matter of minutes and for only a few dollars before contemplating the cost and speed and trouble of moving the exact value of gold in the real world.

It certainly makes you think, doesn't it?

And to further highlight the coming revolution that cryptocurrency will bring to global financial transactions, in 2022, banks and financial institutions globally will migrate from the legacy SWIFT financial messaging system to the highly structured and data-rich ISO 20022 standard.

SWIFT (short for The Society of Worldwide Interbank Financial Telecommunication) is used by thousands of banks worldwide to communicate financial transactions securely and to a set standard.

While a massive step forward from its predecessor, the telex transfer system – it now shows its age and has become somewhat of a monopoly in the ways banks can communicate.

ISO 20022 is the new standard for electronic data interchange between financial institutions. And yes, you guessed it correctly, it has been designed for the world of cryptocurrency, with compliant cryptos including Stellar Lumins XLM Ripple XRP and Algorand ALGO, with Ripple also being part of the ISO 20022 management group. And that is very interesting, too, given the current SEC court case against Ripple labs in the US.

So again, a simple question.

Why would the financial establishment be designing and switching to a new future-facing, indeed a cryptocurrency-friendly protocol if it does not see the future as cryptocurrency?

Answers on a postcard please, as they used to say!

And thirdly, not only do we have two-thirds of the world governments developing forms of cryptocurrency, the financial establishment moving to a new crypto-friendly standard, but we also find many of the world's wealthiest and most influential men and women banging the revolutionary drum too.

Elon musk is a regular commentator on all things crypto and is well documented in his views that it represents the future.

At the same time, recently, we saw Jack Dorsey, the American tech entrepreneur and co-founder of Twitter, quit his role as CEO and go all-in on cryptocurrency.

And if that doesn't convince you that the platform age is about to be swept away by the cryptocurrency revolution and a new, improved internet built around web3, then perhaps listen to my teenage son Finlay.

Recently turned 17, Finlay doesn't really use social media and has never been near Facebook as it is only for 'old farts' like me.

However, he is all in on the metaverse and web3 and critically receives his allowance monthly in Bitcoin XLM and XRP.

Yes, unlike me, he is one smart kid.

Now usually, at this point in any discussion around cryptocurrency, people badger me to end with my own cryptocurrency recommendations and preferences.

But I am not going to do that here.

Not because using the well-worn crypto influencer is 'not financial advice,' nor because I don't believe in the cryptocurrency revolution, which hopefully by now you realize I entirely do.

But instead, as with anything worthwhile in life, the only way to really embrace and understand something, I believe, is to dive in and get involved yourself.

And hopefully, after having read my story of Gold, Greed, and Good, that is something you know I intend to do.

So, if not through sharing my cryptocurrency tips, how then to end this book?

Well, that is easy. Let's end where we started, with this anonymous, Beatles-inspired wisdom delivered by an unknown graffiti artist, presumably at some point in the last year.

"If money can't buy your love, maybe bitcoin can."

Well, I guess we shall soon see.

Thank you for reading.

Printed in Great Britain
by Amazon

78461711R00078